A Heart Of Conviction

Joshua Rhoades

Published by Joshua Paul Rhoades, 2024.

A HEART OF CONVICTION

First edition. October 5, 2024.

ISBN: 979-8227153753

Written by Joshua Rhoades.

Also by Joshua Rhoades

Courage Under Fire: David's Stand On The Battlefield
Jonah's Journey: Voices Of Redemption And Lessons In Obedience
The Furnace Of Faith: 12 Principles From The Heat Of Faith
Whispers of Hope: Inspiring Stories of Men's Prayers In Scripture
Frontier Legends: The Oregon Dream
Elijah: A Beacon Of Boldness
HOOK, LINE & SAVIOUR - Faith Reflections from Fishing
Driven By Faith: Motor Racing Inspired Christian Life
30 Day Devotional - Bold and Strong- Coffee Devotions for a Courageous Christian Walk
Authentic Christianity: The Heart of Old Time Religion
Consider The Ant - God's Tiny Preachers
Flee Fornication: The Plea For Purity
Renewed Hope- How to Find Encouragement in God
Sounding The Call - The Voice of Conviction
The Altar - Where Heaven Meets Earth
The Bible's Battlefields- Timeless Lessons from Ancient Wars
The Sacred Art of Silence - How Silence Speaks in Scripture
Under Fire- The Sanctity of the Traditional Biblical Home
Who Is on the Lord's Side? A Call to Righteousness
What Is Truth? - From Skepticism to Submission
First and Goal- Faith and Football Fundamentals
From Dugout to Devotion- Spiritual Lessons from Baseball
Par for the Course- Faith and Fairways
The Believer's Pace- Tools for Running Life's Marathon
The Immutable Fortress- Security in God's Unchanging Nature
Biblical Bravery
Deer Stands and Devotions: A Hunter's Walk with God

Dedication

To you, the reader,

This book, "A Heart of Conviction", is dedicated to you. Whether you picked it up out of curiosity, a desire to grow in your faith, or because you feel the weight of today's challenges, I want you to know this: you are not alone in this journey. In a world that often feels overwhelming, filled with distractions, pressures, and a constant pull to compromise, living with conviction can seem like an impossible task. But as you'll see throughout these pages, living a life of conviction, just like Daniel did, is not only possible—it's essential.

The days we are living in demand a heart that is fully committed to God. Each day presents us with choices—choices about how we will live, what we will stand for, and who we will follow. Will we follow the world's ever-changing values, or will we stand firm in our faith? Will we bend under the pressure to conform, or will we purpose in our hearts, like Daniel, to honor God no matter the cost?

This book is not just about learning how Daniel stood firm; it's about how you can live with the same bold faith today. You may face situations that test your integrity, moments where the easy path seems tempting, or times when it feels like you're standing alone. But this is where conviction comes in—the kind of conviction that says, "I will not waver. I will trust God and follow His ways, even when it's hard."

The days we are living in are uncertain, but that's all the more reason why a heart of conviction is needed. This book is dedicated to helping you find the strength to stand firm, to encourage you to make the decision to live for God fully, and to inspire you to press forward with faith, knowing that God is with you in every step of your journey.

As you read these pages, I hope you feel challenged, but more importantly, I hope you feel encouraged. You are capable of living a life of conviction, no matter what the world throws your way. And the best part? You don't have to do it on your own. Just as God was with Daniel, guiding him, protecting him, and giving him the courage to stay true to his faith, God is with you too.

May this book remind you that you are called to something greater than the passing trends of this world. You are called to stand for truth, to live for God, and to be a light in the darkness. "A Heart of Conviction" is not just a book—it's a guide for living boldly, courageously, and faithfully in these uncertain times.

With this dedication, I pray that you will find the strength and courage to live with unwavering conviction, trusting that God is with you every step of the way.

Introduction

In a world full of distractions and pressures to conform, standing firm in our faith can seem difficult, if not impossible. We face daily challenges that test our beliefs, tempt us to compromise, and pull us away from the values we know to be true. The story of Daniel, found in the Bible, offers a powerful example of what it means to have a heart of conviction. In Daniel 1:8, it says, "But Daniel purposed in his heart that he would not defile himself with the portion of the king's meat, nor with the wine which he drank." This verse tells us that Daniel made a clear and firm decision in his heart to stay faithful to God, even when he was surrounded by temptation and pressure to do otherwise.

Daniel's choice wasn't easy. He was a young man in a foreign land, living under the rule of a powerful king who expected him to conform to the ways of Babylon. Yet Daniel resolved not to defile himself by eating food that was against God's commandments. This decision could have cost him his place in the king's court or even his life, but Daniel chose to remain true to his faith. His courage, determination, and unwavering commitment to God set him apart as a man of conviction.

"A Heart of Conviction" is inspired by Daniel's life and his bold decision to stand firm in his faith, no matter the cost. This book will challenge you to examine your own faith and consider whether you, like Daniel, are willing to purpose in your heart to stay faithful to God, even when the world pressures you to compromise. In today's culture, where we are constantly tempted to fit in, follow the crowd, or choose the easier path, we need the same heart of conviction that Daniel had.

This book is a call to live with unwavering faith, to make decisions based on God's truth, and to trust that God will honor our commitment to Him, just as He did with Daniel. It's about standing firm in the face of temptation, pressures, and challenges, knowing that a life of conviction brings glory to God and strength to our souls. "A Heart of Conviction" will encourage you to live boldly for God, to trust in His guidance, and to embrace a faith that is unshakable, no matter the circumstances.

Chapter 1 – Dedication

A heart of conviction, as shown in Daniel's decision to remain faithful to God, reflects a deep dedication that is essential in today's world. The Bible tells us in Daniel 1:8 "But Daniel purposed in his heart that he would not defile himself," which means that Daniel made a strong and firm decision in his heart to stay true to God, despite the pressures around him. This kind of dedication is important for all believers today because we live in a world that constantly challenges our faith, values, and beliefs. Society often tries to push us in different directions, tempting us to compromise on what we believe or to follow the crowd, but Daniel's example shows us that we must remain committed to God no matter what. Dedication to God means staying firm in our beliefs, even when it's hard, even when everyone else is doing something different, and even when we face opposition or pressure to change. Daniel was living in a foreign land, surrounded by a culture that did not honor God, but he purposed in his heart that he would stay faithful. This kind of dedication is needed now more than ever, because today, we too live in a world that is often hostile to faith. Many people are focused on materialism, power, and personal success, and it can be tempting to follow the world's path instead of staying true to God. But Daniel's story reminds us that dedication to God must come first, no matter the circumstances. He was dedicated to following God's laws and commands, and he refused to defile himself with the king's food and wine. This was a difficult decision, because refusing the king's provisions could have brought Daniel into danger, but his heart was set on pleasing God above all else. Dedication to God means putting Him first, even when it's risky, even when it costs us something, and even when we don't know what the outcome will be. Daniel's dedication was not just about following rules; it was about a deep commitment to honoring God with his life. This is what dedication truly means – it's about more than just outward actions, it's about the condition of our heart. Daniel's heart was fully devoted to God, and that is what gave him the strength to stand firm in his convictions. Today, we are often faced with situations where our faith is tested. We might be pressured to do things that go against our beliefs, or we might be tempted to compromise in order to fit in or avoid conflict. But if we have a heart of conviction like Daniel, we will stay true to God, no matter what the world throws at us. A heart of conviction means that our faith is not just something we talk about or something we show in public, but it's something that truly guides every decision we make. It means that we are dedicated to following God in every area of our lives, not just when it's easy or convenient. Daniel's dedication to God was not a one-time decision; it was a daily choice to honor God in everything he did. Even in the small things, like the food he ate, Daniel remained faithful to God. This teaches us that dedication to God is shown not just in big moments, but in the everyday decisions we make. It's about living a life that is fully surrendered to God, in every aspect. When we have a heart of conviction, like Daniel, we will be able to resist the pressures of the world and stay true to our faith. Daniel's dedication is a powerful example for us today because we live in a world that often promotes values that are contrary to the Bible. Whether it's in the media, in school, at work, or in social situations, we are constantly bombarded with messages that tell us to put ourselves first, to seek after wealth or success, or to compromise our beliefs in order to fit in. But Daniel's story reminds us that dedication to God means standing firm in our faith, even when it's not popular, even when it's difficult, and even when it sets us apart from others. Dedication to God is about living a life that reflects His truth and His love, no matter what others may say or think. It's about being willing to stand alone if necessary, just as Daniel did. Daniel's dedication to God was rewarded because God honored his faithfulness. God gave Daniel wisdom, understanding, and favor with the king, but Daniel's dedication was not about seeking rewards; it was about his deep love and commitment to God. This is the kind of dedication we need today – a dedication that is not based on what we can get from God, but on a desire to honor Him and live for Him. A heart of conviction means that our faith is not dependent on our circumstances, but on our relationship with God. Daniel remained dedicated to God even when he was far from home, even when he was in a foreign land, and even when he faced the possibility of danger. This shows us that dedication to God is not about where we are or what's happening around us; it's about who we are in Christ. Today, we might face challenges to our faith, but if we have a heart of conviction, we will be able to stand strong, just as Daniel did. We need to be dedicated to God in every area of our lives, whether it's in our personal relationships, our work, our entertainment choices, or the way we spend our time. Dedication to God means seeking His will in everything we do, and being willing to follow Him wherever He leads, even when it's difficult. Daniel's story reminds us that dedication to God is a daily decision – it's about purposing in our hearts, just as Daniel did, to live a life that honors God. This kind of dedication is needed now more than ever because we live in a world that is constantly trying to pull us away from God. But if we have a heart of conviction, we will be able to stand firm in our faith, no matter what challenges come our way. Dedication to God is not always easy, but it is always worth it, because when we are dedicated to God, He will guide us, protect us, and give us the strength we need to stay true to Him. In the end, Daniel's story is a powerful reminder that a heart of conviction is one of the most important things we can have as believers. It's what gives us the strength to stay faithful to God, no matter what the world throws at us, and it's what helps us live a life that truly honors Him.

Chapter 2 – Discipline

A heart of conviction, as shown through Daniel's life in the Bible, required a great deal of discipline, especially in a world full of distractions and temptations. In Daniel 1:8, it says, "But Daniel purposed in his heart that he would not defile himself with the portion of the king's meat, nor with the wine which he drank." This simple yet powerful decision reveals how Daniel was disciplined in his faith and in his commitment to God. Daniel lived in Babylon, a foreign land with a culture that was very different from his own, one that did not honor God. He was surrounded by temptations—luxuries, food, power, and opportunities to gain favor with the king. Yet, Daniel remained steadfast in his choice to obey God's laws, even when it would have been easier to give in and follow the crowd. This level of discipline is something we all need today because we, too, live in a world full of distractions and temptations that can easily pull us away from God.

Discipline is the ability to control one's actions, thoughts, and desires in order to achieve a higher goal. For Daniel, that goal was to remain pure and obedient to God. He didn't want to compromise his faith or his relationship with God by indulging in things that went against God's commands. This kind of discipline isn't easy. It requires a constant effort to stay focused on what truly matters, especially when the world offers so many alternatives that may seem easier or more appealing. Daniel's discipline allowed him to resist the temptations around him, and it is a lesson that applies to us today. We, too, must be disciplined in our faith if we want to maintain a strong relationship with God. This means resisting the things that can lead us astray, such as materialism, pride, selfishness, or anything that distracts us from living a life that honors God.

In today's world, there are countless distractions—social media, entertainment, peer pressure, the pursuit of success and recognition—that can tempt us to stray from our faith or compromise our values. Discipline helps us stay grounded in our beliefs, just as Daniel did. He knew what was right in God's eyes, and he chose to stick to it, even when it meant going against the norm or standing out. Daniel didn't conform to the culture around him; instead, he remained disciplined in following God's commands. This teaches us that discipline in our faith is not about following the trends of society but about staying true to what God has called us to do.

One of the greatest challenges we face today is staying disciplined in a world that constantly encourages instant gratification. Whether it's through technology, media, or societal expectations, we are often tempted to take shortcuts or seek quick satisfaction. But Daniel's life shows us that true discipline involves patience, self-control, and long-term commitment to our faith. He didn't look for quick fixes or shortcuts; instead, he trusted in God's plan and remained disciplined in his decisions. This is something we need to remember today. Discipline means being able to say no to the things that might feel good in the moment but will ultimately pull us away from God's purpose for our lives. It means being able to stay focused on what really matters, even when the world offers us easier or more tempting paths.

Daniel's discipline also involved his daily habits. He prayed regularly, sought God's wisdom, and lived according to God's Word. Discipline in faith is not just about resisting temptation; it's about building good habits that strengthen our relationship with God. Just as Daniel made it a point to stay connected to God through prayer, we too need to develop spiritual disciplines, like reading the Bible, praying, and spending time with God, in order to stay strong in our faith. These spiritual habits help us to stay focused on God's will for our lives and prevent us from being swayed by the distractions and temptations around us. When we are disciplined in our spiritual practices, we are better equipped to face the challenges of life and remain faithful to God.

Discipline in faith is also about being consistent. Daniel didn't waver in his decision to stay pure. Once he made the choice to honor God, he stuck to it, no matter what came his way. Today, it's easy to be disciplined for a short period of time but then lose focus or get discouraged when things get difficult. Daniel's story reminds us that discipline is not just a one-time decision—it's an ongoing commitment to stay true to God every day, in every situation. It requires consistency and perseverance, even when it's hard or when others around us are choosing a different path. Discipline helps us to stay committed to our faith, no matter what challenges or temptations we face.

Another important aspect of discipline that Daniel demonstrated is the ability to prioritize God's will above all else. Discipline in faith means putting God first, even when other things seem more urgent or attractive. Daniel was in a position where he could have easily focused on pleasing the king or gaining favor in the royal court, but he chose instead to please God. This teaches us that discipline in faith means choosing God's will over our own desires or the desires of others. It's about making decisions that honor God, even when they go against what the world expects or values. Discipline helps us to keep our priorities in order, making sure that God always comes first in our lives.

Discipline also requires self-control, which is something Daniel demonstrated throughout his life. He didn't let his circumstances control his decisions; instead, he remained in control of his actions by choosing to follow God's commands. Self-control is a key part of discipline because it helps us resist the temptations that can lead us away from God. In today's world, where we are constantly bombarded with messages that encourage us to indulge in whatever we want, self-control is more important than ever. It helps us to stay focused on what is right and to avoid the things that can harm our relationship with God. Just as Daniel was able to control his desires and stay true to his faith, we too need to practice self-control in order to live a life that honors God.

Another lesson we learn from Daniel's discipline is the importance of making decisions ahead of time. Daniel didn't wait until he was faced with temptation to decide whether or not he would obey God—he had already purposed in his heart that he would not defile himself. This kind of discipline means making a firm decision to follow God before we are faced with temptation. When we purpose in our hearts to stay true to God, it becomes easier to resist the temptations that come our way because we've already made up our minds. This is a powerful lesson for us today, as we are constantly faced with decisions that test our faith. Discipline helps us to make the right choices ahead of time, so that when temptation comes, we are ready to stand firm in our faith.

Daniel's discipline also teaches us the value of accountability. While Daniel made the decision to stay pure, he wasn't alone in his efforts. His friends, Shadrach, Meshach, and Abednego, also chose to stay true to God, and together they were able to support and encourage one another in their faith. This shows us that discipline in faith is often strengthened when we have others around us who share our convictions. Today, it's important to surround ourselves with people who encourage us in our faith and hold us accountable to living a life that honors God. When we have a community of believers to support us, it becomes easier to stay disciplined in our faith, even when we face challenges or temptations.

In conclusion, Daniel's ability to purpose in his heart required strong discipline, and his example teaches us important lessons about how to maintain a life of faith in a world full of distractions and temptations. Discipline helps us to stay focused on God's will, resist temptation, and remain committed to our faith, no matter what challenges come our way. It requires self-control, consistency, and the ability to prioritize God's will above all else. Just as Daniel remained disciplined in his faith, we too need to develop spiritual disciplines that strengthen our relationship with God and help us to stay true to our convictions. Today, discipline is needed more than ever, as we navigate a world that constantly pulls us away from God. By following Daniel's example and staying disciplined in our faith, we can live a life that honors God and remain faithful to Him, no matter what distractions or temptations come our way.

Chapter 3 – Determination

A heart of conviction, as shown by Daniel, is deeply rooted in determination, and his unwavering determination to follow God's commandments is a key lesson for us today. In Daniel 1:8, it says, "But Daniel purposed in his heart that he would not defile himself with the portion of the king's meat, nor with the wine which he drank." This verse tells us that Daniel made a firm decision in his heart to follow God's commandments, even though he was in a foreign land, surrounded by people who didn't share his beliefs. Daniel's determination wasn't just about saying he believed in God—it was about living out those beliefs every day, no matter what challenges or temptations came his way. His determination to stay faithful to God, despite the pressures around him, is a powerful example of what it means to have a heart of conviction. Today, we live in a world that is full of external pressures. Whether it's peer pressure, societal expectations, or the constant influence of media and culture, it's easy to feel like we are being pulled in different directions. Sometimes, it might even feel easier to just go along with what everyone else is doing rather than standing firm in our faith. But Daniel's example shows us that determination is crucial if we want to live a faithful life and uphold godly values. Daniel didn't waver in his decision to follow God's commandments, even when he faced difficult circumstances. He was taken to Babylon, a place where the people did not honor or serve the God of Israel, and where the king's orders were the law. Yet, Daniel purposed in his heart that he would not defile himself with the king's food and drink, which went against the dietary laws given by God. This decision wasn't just about food; it was about staying faithful to God's Word and honoring Him, even when it was hard. Daniel's determination to obey God, even when it could have put him at risk, teaches us the importance of staying true to our beliefs, no matter what. In today's world, being determined to uphold godly values is more important than ever. We are constantly faced with situations where our faith is tested. Whether it's at school, at work, or in social situations, there are times when it might seem easier to compromise or to follow the crowd. But determination means making a firm decision to follow God's commandments, no matter what pressures we face. It means standing strong in our faith, even when it's not popular or when others might not understand. Daniel's determination wasn't something that just happened in a moment—it was a decision he made in his heart, a commitment to follow God, no matter what challenges came his way. That kind of determination is what we need today. We need to purpose in our hearts, just as Daniel did, to stay faithful to God, even when the world around us seems to be going in the opposite direction. Determination is about having a mindset that is focused on God's will and His commandments. It's about making a choice to live according to God's Word, even when it's difficult or inconvenient. Daniel's story teaches us that determination isn't just about one big decision; it's about the everyday choices we make to follow God. Each time Daniel refused to eat the king's food or drink the wine, he was making a decision to stay faithful to God. Each time he prayed or sought God's guidance, he was showing his determination to follow God's commandments. This teaches us that determination is built through the small, everyday decisions we make to honor God in our lives. In a world that often promotes values that are contrary to the Bible, it can be challenging to stay determined to follow godly values. But Daniel's story reminds us that determination is about staying committed to what we know is right, even when it's hard. It's about choosing to follow God, even when the world is trying to pull us in a different direction. Daniel's determination was rooted in his relationship with God. He knew God's commandments, and he was determined to obey them, no matter what. This teaches us that in order to have the same kind of determination, we need to stay close to God and be grounded in His Word. The more we know God's Word, the more we will be able to stand firm in our faith, just like Daniel did. Determination also requires courage. Daniel's decision to refuse the king's food and drink could have put him in danger, yet he was willing to take that risk because he was determined to follow God's commandments. Today, we may not face the same kind of dangers, but there are still times when standing up for our faith requires courage. It might mean being different from those around us, or it might mean making sacrifices in order to stay faithful to God. But Daniel's example shows us that determination, combined with courage, helps us to stay true to our convictions, no matter what challenges come our way. Another important lesson we learn from Daniel's determination is that it brings blessings. Because Daniel stayed faithful to God, even in the face of pressure, God blessed him with wisdom, understanding, and favor in the eyes of the king. This doesn't mean that following God's commandments will always lead to immediate rewards, but it does show us that when we are determined to stay faithful to God, He will be with us and guide us through whatever challenges we face. Determination doesn't mean that life will always be easy, but it does mean that we can trust in God's faithfulness and know that He will honor our commitment to Him. Today, being determined to follow God's commandments means being intentional about how we live our lives. It means making decisions based on what God's Word says, rather than on what the world says. It means staying true to our beliefs, even when we are tempted to compromise or to take the easy way out. Daniel's determination teaches us that living a faithful life requires focus, commitment, and a willingness to stand strong in our convictions, no matter what pressures we face. Determination is about making a firm decision to follow God, and then sticking to that decision, even when it's hard. It's about trusting that God's commandments are good and that following them will lead to a life that honors Him. Daniel's story is a powerful reminder that determination is essential if we want to live a life of faith. In conclusion, Daniel's unwavering determination to follow God's commandments is a key lesson for us today. In a world that constantly tries to pull us away from godly values, determination is crucial for staying faithful to God. It's about making a firm decision in our hearts, just like Daniel did, to follow God's commandments, no matter what challenges or pressures come our way. Determination helps us to stay focused on God's will, to live according to His Word, and to remain faithful, even when it's difficult. Daniel's example teaches us that when we are determined to follow God, He will guide us, give us strength, and bless us for our faithfulness. Today, we need the same kind of determination that Daniel had—a determination to stand firm in our faith, to honor God in every area of our lives, and to follow His commandments, no matter what.

Chapter 4 - Decision-Making

A heart of conviction, as seen in Daniel's life, is deeply connected to the decisions we make every day, and Daniel's purposeful choices show us the importance of making godly decisions. In Daniel 1:8, it says, "But Daniel purposed in his heart that he would not defile himself with the portion of the king's meat, nor with the wine which he drank." This verse highlights how Daniel made a deliberate, purposeful choice to follow God's commandments, even though he was living in a foreign land where the culture and customs were very different from what he had known. Daniel was a young man, living in Babylon, surrounded by influences that could have easily led him away from his faith, but he made the decision to honor God above all else. This decision was not made lightly—it was a reflection of Daniel's deep commitment to God, and it set the course for the rest of his life. His decision not only kept him faithful to God in that moment, but it also shaped his character, his reputation, and his faith journey in the years to come. Today, we live in a world where we are constantly faced with decisions—some big, some small—but each decision we make has the potential to shape our lives and our relationship with God. Just like Daniel, we need to make purposeful, godly decisions every day, because those decisions reflect our commitment to God and help us grow in our faith.

Daniel's decision not to eat the king's food may seem like a small thing, but it was actually a very significant decision. The king's food was likely offered to idols, and eating it would have meant compromising Daniel's faith and breaking the dietary laws given to him by God. By making the choice not to eat the food, Daniel was standing up for what he believed in, even though it could have cost him his position or even his life. This shows us that making godly decisions isn't always easy—sometimes it requires us to stand out or to go against what everyone else is doing. But Daniel's example teaches us that when we make decisions based on our faith, we are honoring God, and He will be with us, guiding us and giving us the strength we need to follow through. Decision-making is a crucial part of living a faithful life, and each decision we make is an opportunity to either grow closer to God or to drift further away from Him.

In today's world, we are constantly bombarded with choices. From the way we spend our time to the things we watch or listen to, the people we surround ourselves with, and even the words we speak—each of these decisions has the power to influence our lives and shape our character. Daniel's story reminds us that we need to be intentional about the decisions we make. We can't just go along with what everyone else is doing or make decisions based on what feels good in the moment. Instead, we need to make decisions that honor God and reflect our faith. This requires wisdom, prayer, and a heart that is fully committed to following God's will. Daniel didn't make his decision lightly—he purposed in his heart to follow God, which means he made a deliberate, thoughtful choice based on his understanding of God's commandments. This teaches us that when it comes to making decisions, we need to take the time to seek God's guidance, to consider what His Word says, and to make choices that align with His will.

Making godly decisions is not always easy, especially when we are surrounded by a world that often promotes values that are contrary to what the Bible teaches. There will be times when making a godly decision means going against the crowd, just as Daniel did. It might mean standing up for what is right, even when it's unpopular, or choosing to do what pleases God, even when it's difficult. But Daniel's story shows us that when we are faithful in our decisions, God is with us. Daniel's decision not to defile himself with the king's food led to him finding favor with the king and being blessed with wisdom and understanding. This doesn't mean that making godly decisions will always lead to immediate rewards, but it does show us that when we honor God in our choices, He will honor our faithfulness and guide us along the right path.

Our decisions don't just affect us in the moment—they have a lasting impact on our lives. Daniel's decision to follow God in that moment set the tone for the rest of his life. Throughout the book of Daniel, we see how his faithfulness and his commitment to making godly decisions allowed him to be used by God in powerful ways. From interpreting dreams to standing firm in the face of persecution, Daniel's life was marked by a series of godly decisions that reflected his unwavering commitment to God. This teaches us that the decisions we make today can shape the course of our future. When we choose to follow God's commandments and make decisions that honor Him, we are laying the foundation for a life that is rooted in faith, integrity, and purpose.

One of the key lessons we learn from Daniel's decision-making is the importance of being intentional. Daniel didn't just go along with what everyone else was doing—he made a purposeful choice to follow God. This kind of intentional decision-making is crucial in today's world, where it's easy to get swept up in the busyness of life and make decisions without thinking about their impact. But Daniel's story shows us that we need to be purposeful in our decisions, taking the time to consider how each choice we make aligns with our faith and our commitment to God. This requires us to be mindful of the decisions we are making and to seek God's guidance in everything we do. Whether it's a big decision, like choosing a career path, or a small decision, like how we spend our free time, each choice matters because it reflects our heart and our priorities.

Another important aspect of decision-making that we learn from Daniel is the importance of conviction. Daniel didn't make his decision based on what was convenient or easy—he made his decision based on his conviction that following God's commandments was the right thing to do. This teaches us that when it comes to making godly decisions, we need to have a strong conviction in our hearts. We need to know what we believe and why we believe it, and we need to be willing to stand firm in those beliefs, even when it's hard. Having a heart of conviction means that we are not easily swayed by the opinions or pressures of others, but that we are rooted in our faith and committed to making decisions that honor God.

Decision-making is also about responsibility. Daniel took responsibility for his actions and his choices, and he didn't try to shift the blame or make excuses. This teaches us that when we make decisions, we need to take ownership of the choices we make and the consequences that come with them. Sometimes, making a godly decision might lead to challenges or difficulties, but Daniel's story reminds us that when we take responsibility for our actions and trust in God, He will be with us, guiding us through whatever challenges we face.

In conclusion, Daniel's purposeful choice to follow God's commandments teaches us the importance of making godly decisions. In today's world, where we are constantly faced with choices, it is crucial that we make decisions that reflect our commitment to God and align with His will. Just like Daniel, we need to be intentional, thoughtful, and purposeful in our decisions, seeking God's guidance and trusting in His plan for our lives. Each decision we make has the power to shape our character, our faith journey, and our relationship with God. When we make godly decisions, we are honoring God, growing in our faith, and setting the foundation for a life that is rooted in His truth. Daniel's story reminds us that making the right decisions is not always easy, but when we purpose in our hearts to follow God, He will be with us, guiding us, strengthening us, and blessing us along the way. A heart of conviction means making decisions that honor God, even when it's difficult, and trusting that He will lead us on the right path.

Chapter 5 – Devotion

A heart of conviction, as demonstrated by Daniel, reflects an unwavering devotion to God, and his actions throughout his life show us what true devotion looks like. In the book of Daniel, we see how Daniel made choices that always put God first, regardless of the pressures and challenges around him. In Daniel 1:8, it says, "But Daniel purposed in his heart that he would not defile himself with the portion of the king's meat, nor with the wine which he drank." This simple yet powerful decision shows Daniel's deep devotion to God, a devotion that went beyond words and was shown through his actions. Daniel was living in Babylon, a foreign land where the culture and traditions were very different from his own. He was surrounded by people who did not worship the God of Israel and who followed different customs, including eating food that was not in accordance with God's laws. But Daniel's devotion to God was so strong that he refused to defile himself, even though doing so could have made his life easier or helped him gain favor with the king. This kind of devotion is what is needed today, in a world that is fast-paced, focused on self, and often encourages us to prioritize our own desires above God's will.

In today's world, devotion to God is more important than ever because we are constantly surrounded by distractions and influences that can pull us away from Him. Whether it's the busyness of daily life, the pressure to succeed, or the constant focus on material possessions and personal gain, it's easy to get caught up in the world's values and forget about what really matters. But Daniel's life teaches us that true devotion to God means putting Him first in every area of our lives. It means making decisions that reflect our commitment to Him, even when it's hard or when we're surrounded by people who don't share our faith.

Daniel's actions show us that devotion to God is not just about saying we believe in Him—it's about living a life that honors Him in everything we do.

One of the key ways Daniel showed his devotion to God was through his commitment to prayer. Throughout his life, Daniel prayed regularly and sought God's guidance in all things. Even when a decree was issued that forbade anyone from praying to any god or man except the king, Daniel remained faithful. In Daniel 6:10, it says, "Now when Daniel knew that the writing was signed, he went into his house; and his windows being open in his chamber toward Jerusalem, he kneeled upon his knees three times a day, and prayed, and gave thanks before his God, as he did aforetime." This verse shows that Daniel's devotion to God was unwavering, even in the face of persecution. He didn't hide his faith or try to compromise to avoid conflict. Instead, he continued to pray and honor God, just as he always had. This kind of devotion is needed today because we live in a world where it can be tempting to keep our faith private or to compromise in order to fit in with the people around us. But Daniel's example shows us that true devotion to God means staying faithful, even when it's not easy or when it comes with a cost.

Another way Daniel showed his devotion to God was through his obedience to God's commandments. From a young age, Daniel was committed to following God's laws, even when it meant going against the culture around him. His decision not to eat the king's food was not just about following dietary laws—it was about remaining faithful to God and not compromising his beliefs, even in small things. This teaches us that devotion to God is about more than just the big decisions in life—it's about being faithful in the small, everyday choices we make. It's about living a life that is fully surrendered to God's will and making decisions that reflect our desire to honor Him in all things.

In today's fast-paced world, where so many things compete for our attention, it can be easy to lose sight of what's most important. We often find ourselves rushing from one task to the next, focused on our own goals and desires, and neglecting our relationship with God. But Daniel's life teaches us that devotion to God requires intentionality. It means making time for God, seeking Him in prayer, and prioritizing His will above all else. Daniel didn't allow the busyness of life or the pressures of living in a foreign land to distract him from his devotion to God. He remained steadfast in his commitment to following God's commandments and seeking His guidance, even when it would have been easier to go along with the culture around him. This kind of devotion is what we need today if we want to live a life that truly honors God.

Devotion to God is also about trust. Daniel's actions show that he trusted God completely, even when he faced difficult situations. When he was thrown into the lion's den for continuing to pray to God, Daniel didn't panic or try to save himself—he trusted that God would protect him. And God did protect him, closing the mouths of the lions and delivering him from harm. This teaches us that devotion to God means trusting Him, even when we don't understand what's happening or when we're facing challenges. It means believing that God is in control and that He will take care of us, no matter what. Today, we often face uncertainty and challenges, whether it's in our personal lives or in the world around us. But Daniel's example reminds us that devotion to God means trusting Him completely, even when things are difficult.

Devotion to God also requires consistency. Daniel's devotion was not something that changed based on his circumstances—he was devoted to God throughout his entire life, in every situation. Whether he was a young man in Babylon, a high-ranking official in the king's court, or facing persecution for his faith, Daniel's devotion to God remained the same. This teaches us that devotion to God is not something we turn on and off based on what's happening in our lives. It's a constant, ongoing commitment to put God first in everything we do. In today's world, where so many things are constantly changing and demanding our attention, it's easy to lose focus or to let our devotion to God slip. But Daniel's example reminds us that true devotion to God is about being consistent in our faith, no matter what challenges or distractions come our way.

Another important aspect of devotion that we see in Daniel's life is humility. Daniel's devotion to God was not about seeking his own glory or trying to gain power—his focus was always on honoring God. Even when he was given great authority and influence in the king's court, Daniel remained humble, always giving credit to God for his wisdom and success. In Daniel 2:20-21, after God gave Daniel the ability to interpret the king's dream, Daniel said, "Blessed be the name of God for ever and ever: for wisdom and might are his: And he changeth the times and the seasons: he removeth kings, and setteth up kings: he giveth wisdom unto the wise, and knowledge to them that know understanding." This shows that Daniel recognized that everything he had, and everything he was able to do, came from God. This kind of humility is an important part of devotion to God because it reminds us that our lives are not about us—they're about glorifying God. In today's self-centered world, where people often seek recognition and success for themselves, Daniel's humility teaches us that true devotion to God means giving Him the glory in everything we do.

In conclusion, Daniel's actions reflect a heart that was fully devoted to God, and his life teaches us important lessons about what true devotion looks like. In today's fast-paced and self-centered world, where so many things compete for our attention and devotion, Daniel's example reminds us that devotion to God is about prioritizing His will above all else. It's about making time for God, seeking His guidance in prayer, and obeying His commandments, even when it's difficult. It's about trusting God in all circumstances and remaining consistent in our faith, no matter what challenges come our way. Devotion to God is also about humility—recognizing that everything we have comes from Him and giving Him the glory in all that we do. Today, more than ever, we need to have the kind of devotion that Daniel had, a devotion that puts God first in every area of our lives and that reflects a heart that is fully committed to following Him. When we live with this kind of devotion, we will not only grow in our relationship with God, but we will also be able to shine His light in a world that so desperately needs it.

Chapter 6 - Defiance of Sin

A heart of conviction, as demonstrated by Daniel in the Bible, is powerfully reflected in his defiance of sin and his choice to avoid defilement. Daniel's unwavering commitment to avoid defiling himself by partaking in the king's food and wine, as mentioned in Daniel 1:8, teaches us the importance of resisting sin and corruption in a world full of temptations and moral compromises. The verse says, "But Daniel purposed in his heart that he would not defile himself with the portion of the king's meat, nor with the wine which he drank." This decision shows how Daniel was determined to remain pure and faithful to God, despite being in a foreign land where the customs and practices were different from the ones he grew up with. His decision was not an easy one; it took great courage and conviction to stand firm in his faith and resist the pressure to conform. Daniel's example teaches us that defying sin is not only about resisting temptation in the moment, but it's also about making a conscious, purposeful decision to live in a way that honors God, even when the world around us encourages us to compromise our values.

Today, we live in a world that is full of moral compromise. Everywhere we turn, we are faced with messages that encourage us to pursue our own desires, to seek pleasure at any cost, and to ignore God's commands in favor of doing what feels good or seems convenient. Whether it's through the media, peer pressure, or societal expectations, the world often promotes behaviors and attitudes that go against God's Word. In this kind of environment, it can be tempting to give in to sin or to justify actions that we know are wrong. But Daniel's story reminds us that as followers of God, we are called to live differently. We are called to defy sin and to resist the worldly influences that try to pull us away from God.

Defiance of sin requires courage. Daniel's decision to avoid defilement was not without risk. By refusing to eat the king's food and drink the wine, Daniel could have faced punishment or rejection from the king's court. But Daniel was more concerned with pleasing God than with pleasing people. He knew that following God's commandments was more important than gaining favor with the king or fitting in with the culture around him. This kind of courage is what we need today if we are going to stand against sin and worldly corruption. It's not always easy to resist temptation, especially when it feels like everyone else is going along with it. But Daniel's example shows us that true conviction means having the courage to stand up for what is right, even when it's hard or when it comes with a cost.

Defying sin also requires a deep understanding of God's Word. Daniel knew what God's laws said about eating certain foods, and he was committed to following those laws, even in a place where others did not. This teaches us that in order to resist sin, we need to know what God's Word says about how we should live. When we are grounded in Scripture, we are better equipped to recognize sin and to make decisions that honor God. In a world that often promotes values that are contrary to the Bible, it's important for us to be rooted in God's truth so that we can discern right from wrong and make choices that reflect our commitment to living a godly life.

One of the most important lessons we learn from Daniel's defiance of sin is that it's not just about avoiding certain behaviors; it's about maintaining a heart that is pure and focused on God. Daniel's decision to avoid the king's food was about more than just following dietary laws—it was about staying true to his identity as a servant of God and refusing to let the influences of Babylon corrupt his faith. This teaches us that defying sin is about guarding our hearts and minds against the things that can pull us away from God. It's about making intentional choices to stay close to God and to live in a way that reflects His holiness.

In today's world, where sin and corruption are often glamorized or normalized, it can be difficult to maintain a heart of conviction. But Daniel's example shows us that it is possible to live a life that honors God, even in the midst of a corrupt culture. Defying sin doesn't mean isolating ourselves from the world or pretending that we are perfect. It means making a daily decision to choose God's ways over the ways of the world. It means being willing to stand up for what is right, even when it's unpopular or inconvenient. And it means trusting that God will give us the strength we need to resist temptation and to live a life of integrity.

One of the challenges we face today is that sin is often disguised as something harmless or even desirable. The world tells us that certain behaviors are acceptable, even when they go against God's Word. But Daniel's story reminds us that we cannot allow the world's standards to dictate how we live. We must always look to God's Word as our guide and be willing to defy sin, even when it's presented as something that everyone else is doing or something that seems harmless. Daniel's choice to avoid defilement teaches us that living a life of conviction requires us to be discerning and to stay focused on God's truth, rather than being swayed by the world's opinions or trends.

Defying sin also involves accountability. Daniel wasn't alone in his decision to avoid the king's food—his friends Shadrach, Meshach, and Abednego made the same choice. This shows us the importance of surrounding ourselves with people who share our convictions and who can encourage us to stay strong in our faith. When we are accountable to others and when we have a community of believers to support us, it becomes easier to resist temptation and to defy sin. Today, it's important for us to build relationships with other Christians who can help us stay focused on God and who can hold us accountable in our walk with Him.

Another key aspect of defying sin is humility. Daniel's decision to avoid defilement was not about proving that he was better than anyone else—it was about honoring God. This teaches us that when we defy sin, it should come from a place of humility, not pride. It's easy to fall into the trap of thinking that we are more righteous than others because we resist certain temptations, but Daniel's example reminds us that our focus should always be on pleasing God, not on elevating ourselves. Defying sin is about staying true to God's commandments and seeking to live a life that reflects His holiness, not about trying to prove our own moral superiority.

In conclusion, Daniel's choice to avoid defilement teaches us the value of defying sin and worldly corruption. In a world that is full of moral compromise and temptation, we need the courage to stand against sin, just as Daniel did. Defying sin requires a heart of conviction, a deep commitment to following God's Word, and the courage to resist the pressures of the world. It's about making intentional choices to live a life that honors God and reflects His holiness. In today's fast-paced and self-centered world, where sin is often disguised as something desirable or acceptable, Daniel's example reminds us that we must always look to God's Word as our guide and be willing to stand firm in our faith, even when it's difficult. Defying sin is not about isolating ourselves or pretending that we are perfect—it's about staying close to God, guarding our hearts and minds against the influences of the world, and making daily decisions that reflect our commitment to living a life that pleases Him. When we have a heart of conviction like Daniel, we will have the strength to resist temptation and to live a life that honors God, no matter what challenges or pressures we face.

Chapter 7 – Discernment

A heart of conviction, as demonstrated by Daniel in the Bible, is deeply connected to discernment. Daniel's ability to recognize what was spiritually harmful and choose the right path shows the importance of having discernment in our lives. Discernment is the ability to distinguish between right and wrong, good and evil, and truth and deception according to God's standards. In Daniel 1:8, it says, "But Daniel purposed in his heart that he would not defile himself with the portion of the king's meat, nor with the wine which he drank." Daniel's decision to avoid the king's food and drink was not just about following dietary laws; it was about understanding what was spiritually harmful and choosing to stay pure before God. Daniel showed discernment by recognizing that accepting the king's food would compromise his faith and violate God's commandments. His ability to discern between what would honor God and what would lead him away from God's will is a lesson we need to apply today. In a world that is morally complex, full of competing voices, and often confusing messages, we need to exercise discernment to understand what is right and wrong according to God's standards.

Discernment is crucial in our lives because it helps us navigate a world where sin and righteousness are not always clearly defined by society. The world often presents things that are sinful as acceptable, even desirable, and without discernment, it's easy to be deceived into thinking that certain behaviors or choices are harmless when, in fact, they are spiritually harmful. Just as Daniel was able to recognize what would lead him away from God's will, we must develop the ability to discern what aligns with God's truth and what leads us astray. This requires us to be deeply rooted in God's Word and to seek His guidance in every decision we make. Daniel didn't rely on his own understanding—he sought God's wisdom and followed God's commandments, which gave him the ability to discern what was right and wrong. This teaches us that discernment comes from having a heart that is fully committed to following God and His standards.

One of the challenges we face today is that the world often promotes values that are contrary to God's Word. Whether it's through the media, culture, or even peer pressure, we are constantly exposed to messages that tell us to prioritize ourselves, seek personal success at any cost, or pursue things that may look good on the surface but are harmful to our spiritual well-being. Without discernment, it's easy to get swept up in these messages and to make decisions that lead us away from God's will. Daniel's life shows us that discernment is about recognizing these subtle temptations and choosing to stay faithful to God, even when it goes against what the world is telling us to do.

Discernment also helps us to see beyond the surface and understand the spiritual implications of our decisions. Daniel's choice to avoid the king's food might have seemed like a small thing to others, but he understood that it had deeper spiritual significance. By eating the food that was offered to idols, Daniel would have been participating in something that went against God's commandments. His discernment allowed him to see the spiritual harm in something that might have appeared harmless to others. This teaches us that discernment is not just about recognizing obvious sins; it's about understanding the deeper spiritual consequences of our actions and making decisions that honor God in every area of our lives.

In today's morally complex world, discernment is more important than ever. We are constantly faced with decisions about how to live our lives, what to believe, and how to respond to the challenges we face. Without discernment, it's easy to be influenced by the world's values or to make decisions based on what feels right in the moment, rather than what aligns with God's truth. Daniel's example reminds us that we need to seek God's wisdom in every decision we make. We need to pray for discernment and ask God to guide us in understanding what is right and wrong according to His Word. When we rely on God's wisdom, rather than our own understanding or the opinions of others, we are better able to make decisions that honor Him and protect our spiritual well-being.

Discernment is also about being able to recognize when something is spiritually dangerous, even when it doesn't seem that way on the surface. The world often disguises sin as something attractive or harmless, but discernment allows us to see through the deception and understand the true consequences of our actions. Daniel was able to discern that eating the king's food, while it might have seemed like a small thing, would have led him away from God's will. This teaches us that we need to be vigilant in our spiritual lives and to constantly seek God's guidance in recognizing the things that can harm our relationship with Him. Discernment helps us to stay on the right path and to avoid the subtle temptations that can lead us astray.

Another important aspect of discernment is understanding that it's not just about avoiding sin—it's also about choosing what is good and honoring to God. Daniel's decision to avoid the king's food was not just about saying no to something harmful; it was about choosing to remain pure and faithful to God. This teaches us that discernment is not just about avoiding what is wrong—it's about actively seeking what is right and good. It's about making decisions that reflect our desire to honor God in every area of our lives. When we exercise discernment, we are not just protecting ourselves from sin; we are also choosing to live a life that reflects God's holiness and brings glory to Him.

Discernment also involves humility. Daniel's ability to discern what was spiritually harmful came from his deep reliance on God's wisdom, not his own understanding. He didn't trust in his own abilities or knowledge—he trusted in God's guidance. This teaches us that discernment requires humility and a willingness to acknowledge that we don't have all the answers. We need to be willing to seek God's wisdom and to rely on His truth, rather than trusting in our own judgment or the opinions of others. Discernment is about recognizing that God's ways are higher than our ways, and His thoughts are higher than our thoughts (Isaiah 55:9). When we humble ourselves before God and seek His guidance, we are better able to discern what is right and wrong according to His standards.

Another key lesson we learn from Daniel's discernment is that it requires consistency. Daniel didn't just show discernment in one decision—he consistently sought God's guidance and made choices that reflected his commitment to following God's will throughout his life. Whether it was refusing to eat the king's food, interpreting dreams, or continuing to pray even when it was forbidden, Daniel consistently demonstrated discernment in every situation he faced. This teaches us that discernment is not a one-time decision—it's an ongoing practice that requires us to continually seek God's wisdom and to make choices that align with His Word. In today's world, where we are constantly faced with new challenges and temptations, we need to consistently exercise discernment in every decision we make.

Discernment also involves recognizing the influence of others in our lives. Daniel surrounded himself with friends who shared his convictions and who also made the decision to avoid defilement. This shows us that discernment is not just about our own personal decisions—it's also about being mindful of the people we surround ourselves with and the influences we allow into our lives. Today, we are constantly influenced by the people we interact with, the media we consume, and the culture around us. Discernment helps us to recognize which influences are drawing us closer to God and which ones are leading us away from Him. By surrounding ourselves with people who encourage us in our faith and who share our commitment to following God's will, we are better able to exercise discernment and make decisions that honor Him.

In conclusion, Daniel's life demonstrates the importance of discernment in maintaining a heart of conviction. His ability to recognize what was spiritually harmful and to choose the right path shows us that discernment is essential in navigating a morally complex world. Today, we face many challenges and temptations, and without discernment, it's easy to be led astray by the world's values and opinions. But Daniel's example teaches us that when we seek God's wisdom and rely on His truth, we are able to discern what is right and wrong according to His standards. Discernment is not just about avoiding sin—it's about choosing to live a life that honors God and reflects His holiness. It requires humility, consistency, and a deep reliance on God's Word. In a world where the lines between right and wrong are often blurred, discernment helps us to stay on the right path and to make decisions that bring glory to God. When we have a heart of conviction like Daniel, we are able to exercise discernment in every area of our lives and to live in a way that reflects our commitment to following God's will.

Chapter 8 - Dependence on God

A heart of conviction, as demonstrated by Daniel, reflects a life rooted in total dependence on God. Daniel's ability to stand firm in his decision not to defile himself with the king's food and to remain faithful to God despite the pressures around him reveals how much he relied on God for guidance, wisdom, and strength. In Daniel 1:8, it says, "But Daniel purposed in his heart that he would not defile himself with the portion of the king's meat, nor with the wine which he drank." Daniel's decision was not an easy one. He was a young man, living in a foreign land, far from home, and surrounded by people who did not worship or follow the God of Israel. Despite being offered luxury and privileges in the Babylonian court, Daniel depended on God for the strength to resist the temptation to conform to the culture around him. This dependence on God is a central part of Daniel's heart of conviction, and it is a lesson we must apply in our own lives today. In a world that is filled with distractions, temptations, and challenges, we, too, must cultivate a deep and unwavering dependence on God, trusting Him for wisdom, strength, and guidance in every decision we make.

Daniel's dependence on God was not just about following a set of rules or traditions. It was about having a deep relationship with God and trusting Him in every aspect of his life. Daniel knew that by relying on God, he would be able to make the right choices, even when the pressures around him were immense. His dependence on God gave him the courage to stand up for what he believed in and to remain faithful to God's commandments, even when it meant risking his own safety. This teaches us that when we depend on God, we are not relying on our own strength or wisdom—we are relying on His. Today, we face many challenges in our faith. There are pressures from society, culture, and even from within ourselves to compromise or to take the easier path. But Daniel's story reminds us that when we depend on God, we can stand firm in our convictions, knowing that He will provide the strength we need to remain faithful.

Dependence on God also means trusting Him for wisdom. Daniel didn't rely on his own understanding or the opinions of those around him. He sought God's wisdom in every decision he made, and as a result, God blessed him with understanding and insight that set him apart from others. In Daniel 2, when the king had a troubling dream and none of the wise men could interpret it, Daniel prayed to God for wisdom, and God revealed the meaning of the dream to him. This shows us that when we depend on God for wisdom, He will guide us in the right direction. In our own lives, we often face situations where we don't know what to do or how to respond. But just as Daniel sought God's wisdom, we must also turn to God in prayer, asking Him to give us the discernment we need to make decisions that align with His will. Dependence on God for wisdom is essential because it allows us to see beyond our own limited perspective and to trust in His perfect plan for our lives.

In today's fast-paced and complex world, it can be tempting to rely on our own abilities, knowledge, or resources to navigate through life. But Daniel's example teaches us that true strength and wisdom come from depending on God. He knew that without God's guidance, he could not stand firm in his faith or make the right choices. This dependence on God is something we must cultivate in our own lives. It requires humility and a recognition that we are not in control, but that God is. Daniel's willingness to depend on God, even in the face of danger, shows us the power of trusting in God's sovereignty. In our own lives, we must learn to let go of the need to control every situation and instead place our trust in God, knowing that He is faithful and that His plans for us are good.

Daniel's dependence on God was also evident in his prayer life. Throughout the book of Daniel, we see how Daniel regularly prayed to God, seeking His guidance and strength. Even when a decree was issued that forbade anyone from praying to any god or man except the king, Daniel continued to pray to God, as he had always done. In Daniel 6:10, it says, "Now when Daniel knew that the writing was signed, he went into his house; and his windows being open in his chamber toward Jerusalem, he kneeled upon his knees three times a day, and prayed, and gave thanks before his God, as he did aforetime." This shows us that Daniel's dependence on God was not just in times of crisis—it was a daily practice. He didn't only turn to God when he was in trouble; he sought God's presence and guidance every day. This teaches us that dependence on God is not something we do only in difficult times—it's something we must cultivate in our daily lives. By praying regularly and seeking God's guidance in everything we do, we strengthen our relationship with Him and build a foundation of faith that can withstand the challenges and pressures of life.

Dependence on God also requires trust in His timing. Daniel had to trust that God would work in His own time and in His own way, even when the situation seemed impossible. When Daniel and his friends were thrown into the fiery furnace for refusing to bow down to the king's idol, they trusted that God would deliver them, but they also recognized that even if God did not save them, they would still remain faithful. This teaches us that dependence on God means trusting Him, even when we don't understand His plan or when things don't go the way we expect. It means believing that God is in control and that His ways are higher than our ways. In our own lives, there will be times when we face challenges or situations that seem overwhelming, but just as Daniel and his friends trusted in God's deliverance, we must also place our trust in Him, knowing that He is faithful and that He will never leave us.

Another important aspect of dependence on God is recognizing our own limitations. Daniel understood that he could not accomplish anything on his own—he needed God's strength and guidance. This humility allowed him to fully rely on God and to trust in His power. In today's world, where self-sufficiency and independence are often praised, it can be difficult to admit that we need help. But Daniel's example shows us that true strength comes from recognizing our weakness and turning to God for help. Dependence on God is not a sign of weakness—it is a recognition that we are human and that we need God's strength to live a life of faith. When we depend on God, we are acknowledging that He is the source of all wisdom, strength, and guidance, and we are placing our trust in His ability to lead us.

Dependence on God also means being willing to surrender our own desires and plans to His will. Daniel didn't try to impose his own agenda—he was fully surrendered to God's plan for his life. This teaches us that dependence on God requires us to let go of our own ambitions and to seek God's will above all else. It means being willing to trust that God's plans for us are better than anything we could imagine, even when we don't understand what He is doing. In our own lives, we must learn to surrender our plans to God, trusting that He knows what is best for us and that He will lead us in the right direction.

In conclusion, Daniel's ability to stand firm in his decision not to defile himself and to remain faithful to God demonstrates his complete dependence on God. His life teaches us the importance of cultivating a similar dependence on God in our own lives. In today's world, where we are often tempted to rely on our own abilities, knowledge, or resources, we must learn to trust in God for wisdom, strength, and guidance. Dependence on God requires humility, trust, and a recognition that we are not in control—God is. By seeking God's guidance in prayer, trusting in His timing, and surrendering our own desires to His will, we can develop a heart of conviction that is rooted in complete dependence on God. Just as Daniel relied on God to help him stand firm in his faith, we, too, can depend on God to guide us, strengthen us, and lead us on the path of righteousness.

Chapter 9 - Diligence

A heart of conviction, as demonstrated by Daniel, is deeply connected to diligence. Daniel's persistence in staying true to his faith, even when faced with difficult circumstances, is a powerful example of what it means to have a heart that is committed to God. In Daniel 1:8, it says, "But Daniel purposed in his heart that he would not defile himself with the portion of the king's meat, nor with the wine which he drank." This decision reveals Daniel's determination and diligence in maintaining his faith, even when everything around him was pushing him to conform to the ways of Babylon. Daniel's diligence wasn't just about avoiding defilement—it was about continually seeking to honor God in every area of his life, no matter the challenges he faced. This kind of diligence is something that we desperately need in our lives today. In a time when many people give up easily, when the pressures of life or the distractions of the world can lead us away from our faith, we need to be diligent in our spiritual practices, such as prayer, study of the Word, and obedience to God's commandments. Daniel's life shows us that diligence is key to living a life of conviction, and it is through consistent, faithful efforts that we stay close to God and grow in our relationship with Him.

One of the most remarkable things about Daniel is how he remained diligent in his faith even in the most difficult circumstances. Taken to Babylon as a young man, Daniel was placed in a culture that was completely foreign to him, surrounded by people who did not worship the God of Israel, and immersed in a system that was trying to change his identity and beliefs. Yet, Daniel remained true to God. He didn't waver in his commitment to follow God's commandments, even when it would have been easier to simply go along with what everyone else was doing. This shows us that diligence is not just about working hard—it's about staying faithful to God even when the situation is tough. It's about consistently choosing to follow God, even when we are surrounded by influences that would lead us in the opposite direction. In our world today, we are often bombarded with distractions, pressures, and temptations that can easily pull us away from God. But like Daniel, we need to be diligent in our spiritual lives, remaining faithful to God even when it's difficult, even when the world around us is encouraging us to compromise.

Diligence in faith means being intentional about our spiritual practices. Daniel's commitment to prayer, for example, is one of the clearest demonstrations of his diligence. In Daniel 6:10, it says, "Now when Daniel knew that the writing was signed, he went into his house; and his windows being open in his chamber toward Jerusalem, he kneeled upon his knees three times a day, and prayed, and gave thanks before his God, as he did aforetime." Even when a decree was issued that made it illegal to pray to anyone other than the king, Daniel continued his practice of praying to God three times a day. This shows us that Daniel's diligence was not dependent on his circumstances—whether it was legal or not, whether it was easy or hard, Daniel remained faithful in his practice of prayer. This is the kind of diligence we need in our own spiritual lives. We need to be committed to seeking God in prayer, not just when it's convenient or when we feel like it, but every day, no matter what is happening in our lives. Prayer is one of the most important ways we stay connected to God, and diligence in prayer helps us to remain strong in our faith, even when we are faced with challenges or difficulties.

Diligence is also important when it comes to studying God's Word. Daniel's knowledge of God's laws was one of the reasons he was able to stay faithful in Babylon. He knew what God required of him, and he was committed to following those commandments, even in a foreign land. This teaches us that diligence in studying the Bible is essential for living a life of conviction. If we don't know what God's Word says, we won't be able to make decisions that honor Him. Diligence in studying the Bible means making time to read and meditate on Scripture, seeking to understand God's will for our lives, and applying His truths to our everyday decisions. In today's world, it can be easy to let the busyness of life crowd out time for studying the Bible. But Daniel's example reminds us that we must be diligent in seeking God's Word if we want to grow in our faith and remain strong in our convictions.

Obedience is another key aspect of diligence. Daniel didn't just know God's commandments—he lived them out in his daily life. His decision not to eat the king's food was an act of obedience to God's laws, and his refusal to stop praying was another example of his commitment to obeying God, even when it was dangerous. Diligence in obedience means that we are not just hearers of the Word, but doers as well (James 1:22). It means that we are committed to following God's commandments in every area of our lives, even when it's difficult or when we face opposition. In our lives today, there are many temptations to compromise our obedience to God. Whether it's peer pressure, societal expectations, or personal desires, there are always forces at work that try to pull us away from following God's will. But like Daniel, we must be diligent in our obedience, making the choice to follow God's ways, even when it's not the easy or popular thing to do.

Diligence is also about consistency. Daniel's faithfulness was not a one-time decision—it was a lifelong commitment. Throughout the book of Daniel, we see how he remained faithful to God in every stage of his life, from his time as a young man in Babylon to his position as a high-ranking official in the king's court. This shows us that diligence is not just about making one good decision or being faithful for a short period of time—it's about consistently living out our faith every day. In today's world, where so many things are constantly changing, it can be easy to lose focus or to let our spiritual practices slip. But Daniel's example reminds us that we need to be diligent in our faith, continually seeking to honor God in everything we do, day after day, year after year. Consistency in our spiritual practices, such as prayer, Bible study, and obedience, helps us to grow in our relationship with God and to stay strong in our faith, no matter what challenges or changes we face in life.

Another important aspect of diligence is perseverance. Daniel faced many challenges and trials throughout his life, from being taken captive in Babylon to being thrown into the lion's den for his faith. But through it all, he remained diligent in his commitment to God. He didn't give up when things got tough—he persevered in his faith, trusting that God would be with him and that God's plan would prevail. This teaches us that diligence is not just about working hard or being consistent—it's about having the perseverance to keep going, even when we face obstacles or difficulties. In our lives today, there will be times when we face trials or when our faith is tested. But diligence means that we don't give up or lose heart. It means that we continue to seek God, to trust Him, and to remain faithful to Him, even in the midst of challenges.

Diligence in faith also requires humility. Daniel's success in Babylon, his ability to interpret dreams, and his rise to a position of influence were not things he achieved through his own strength—they were the result of God's favor and guidance. Daniel understood this, and he always gave glory to God for the wisdom and understanding he received. In Daniel 2:20-21, after interpreting the king's dream, Daniel said, "Blessed be the name of God for ever and ever: for wisdom and might are his: And he changeth the times and the seasons: he removeth kings, and setteth up kings: he giveth wisdom unto the wise, and knowledge to them that know understanding." This shows us that diligence in faith is not about relying on our own abilities—it's about depending on God and recognizing that everything we have comes from Him. Humility is a key part of diligence because it keeps us focused on God and reminds us that we need His help in everything we do.

In conclusion, Daniel's diligence in staying true to his faith, even in difficult circumstances, is a powerful example for us today. In a time when many people give up easily or allow the distractions of life to pull them away from their faith, we need to be diligent in our spiritual practices, such as prayer, study of God's Word, and obedience to His commandments. Diligence means being intentional about seeking God, being consistent in our faith, and persevering through challenges and trials. It requires humility, as we recognize that we cannot live a life of conviction without God's help and guidance. Daniel's life shows us that diligence is not just about working hard or being persistent—it's about having a heart that is fully committed to God and that seeks to honor Him in everything we do. When we are diligent in our faith, we grow closer to God, strengthen our relationship with Him, and are better equipped to live a life of conviction, no matter what challenges we face. Just as Daniel remained faithful to God in Babylon, we, too, can remain diligent in our faith, trusting that God will be with us and that He will bless our efforts to live a life that honors Him.

Chapter 10 - Determining Boundaries

A heart of conviction, as demonstrated by Daniel in the Bible, shows the importance of determining clear boundaries in life to avoid defilement and stay true to one's faith. Daniel's choice to set boundaries for himself is one of the most powerful examples in the Bible of how a person of faith can live with integrity in a world that does not always align with their beliefs. In Daniel 1:8, it says, "But Daniel purposed in his heart that he would not defile himself with the portion of the king's meat, nor with the wine which he drank." This decision reveals Daniel's commitment to setting boundaries that would protect his spiritual integrity. Even though Daniel was living in a foreign land, far from home, where the customs and practices were very different from his own, he was determined to stay true to God's commandments. Daniel's decision to not eat the king's food or drink his wine was not simply about following dietary laws; it was about maintaining his faith and purity in a place where everything around him was tempting him to conform to the ways of Babylon. The boundaries Daniel set for himself were a reflection of his heart of conviction, and this is a lesson we need to apply in our own lives today. In a world filled with moral compromise and constant pressure to conform to societal norms, we need to determine clear boundaries for ourselves to protect our faith and integrity.

Determining boundaries is an essential part of living a life of conviction because boundaries help us to stay focused on God's will and avoid the temptations and distractions that can lead us away from Him. Daniel's boundaries were clear—he would not defile himself by eating food that was against God's commandments, and he would not engage in practices that violated his faith. This teaches us that setting boundaries is about more than just avoiding sin—it's about making intentional decisions to live in a way that honors God. In today's world, we are constantly faced with choices about how we live our lives, what we consume, how we spend our time, and who we surround ourselves with. Without clear boundaries, it's easy to be swayed by the influences of the world or to compromise our beliefs for the sake of convenience or acceptance. But Daniel's example shows us that living with conviction means determining ahead of time where we draw the line and committing to those boundaries, no matter what pressures we face.

Setting moral and spiritual boundaries is especially important today because the world around us often promotes values that are contrary to God's Word. From the media we consume to the people we interact with, we are constantly bombarded with messages that encourage us to pursue our own desires, to compromise our values, and to conform to the standards of the world. Without clear boundaries, it's easy to get caught up in these influences and to drift away from our faith. But Daniel's life reminds us that boundaries are not about restricting our freedom—they are about protecting our relationship with God and maintaining our integrity. When we set boundaries, we are choosing to prioritize our faith and our commitment to God over the fleeting pleasures and temptations of the world.

Boundaries also help us to avoid situations that could lead us into sin or compromise. Daniel's decision to avoid the king's food was not just about following rules—it was about staying pure and faithful to God in a place where it would have been easy to give in to temptation. This teaches us that boundaries are about being proactive in protecting our faith. Instead of waiting until we are in a difficult situation to decide how we will respond, we need to determine ahead of time what lines we will not cross. For example, setting boundaries in our relationships, in the way we spend our time, or in the media we consume can help us avoid situations that could weaken our faith or lead us into temptation. Just as Daniel purposed in his heart not to defile himself, we need to purpose in our hearts to live according to God's standards, and setting clear boundaries is one of the ways we do that.

One of the challenges we face today is that the world often blurs the lines between right and wrong, making it difficult to determine what is acceptable and what is not. But Daniel's example teaches us that we must look to God's Word as our guide in setting boundaries. Daniel didn't rely on his own understanding or the opinions of those around him—he relied on God's commandments to determine what was right and wrong. This teaches us that the boundaries we set must be based on God's truth, not on the shifting standards of the world.

When we base our boundaries on God's Word, we can have confidence that we are making choices that honor Him and protect our faith.

Another important aspect of determining boundaries is understanding our own weaknesses. Daniel knew that eating the king's food would compromise his faith, and he made the decision to avoid it. This shows us that boundaries are not just about avoiding obvious sins—they are about recognizing the areas in our lives where we are most vulnerable and setting limits to protect ourselves. For example, if we know that certain behaviors, places, or relationships make it harder for us to stay faithful to God, we need to set boundaries in those areas to protect our spiritual health. This requires humility and self-awareness, as well as a willingness to be honest with ourselves about our limitations. Setting boundaries is not about being rigid or overly cautious—it's about recognizing the importance of protecting our faith and making decisions that keep us close to God.

Boundaries are also about maintaining our identity as followers of Christ. Daniel was living in a foreign land, surrounded by people who did not worship the God of Israel, but he remained true to his identity as one of God's people. By setting boundaries and refusing to conform to the ways of Babylon, Daniel was making a statement about who he was and what he stood for. This teaches us that boundaries are about more than just avoiding sin—they are about maintaining our identity as followers of Christ. In today's world, where there is constant pressure to conform to the values and practices of the culture around us, boundaries help us to stay true to who we are in Christ. They remind us that we are called to be set apart, to live according to God's standards, and to reflect His character in everything we do.

Boundaries also help us to maintain our integrity. Daniel's decision to avoid defilement was not just about following rules—it was about staying true to his convictions and maintaining his integrity, even in a place where it would have been easy to compromise. This teaches us that boundaries are essential for living a life of integrity. When we set clear boundaries, we are making a commitment to live in a way that honors God, even when no one else is watching. Integrity is about being consistent in our faith and our actions, regardless of the circumstances, and boundaries help us to stay true to that commitment. In a world where moral compromise is common and integrity is often overlooked, setting boundaries is one of the ways we protect our integrity and remain faithful to God.

Another key lesson we learn from Daniel's example is that boundaries require courage. Daniel's decision to avoid the king's food was a bold one, and it could have put him at risk of losing his position or even his life. But Daniel was more concerned with pleasing God than with pleasing people, and he had the courage to stand by his convictions, even when it was difficult. This teaches us that setting and maintaining boundaries is not always easy—it requires courage and a willingness to stand firm in our faith, even when others may not understand or agree. In today's world, there will be times when setting boundaries means going against the flow or standing out from the crowd. But Daniel's example shows us that when we have a heart of conviction and are committed to honoring God, we will have the courage to set boundaries and to stand by them, no matter what challenges we face.

Boundaries also help us to stay focused on God's will for our lives. Daniel's decision to avoid defilement was a reflection of his desire to stay true to God's purpose for his life. By setting boundaries, Daniel was able to avoid distractions and temptations that could have pulled him away from God's plan. This teaches us that boundaries are not just about avoiding sin—they are about staying focused on God's will for our lives. When we set clear boundaries, we are creating space in our lives for God to work, and we are positioning ourselves to grow in our relationship with Him. In today's fast-paced and distracted world, boundaries help us to stay focused on what truly matters—our relationship with God and our commitment to following His will.

In conclusion, Daniel's decision to determine clear boundaries for himself to avoid defilement is a powerful example of how we can live with conviction in a world that is often filled with moral compromise. Setting boundaries is essential for protecting our faith and maintaining our integrity in a world that constantly encourages us to conform to its standards. Boundaries help us to stay focused on God's will, avoid temptation, and maintain our identity as followers of Christ. They require courage, humility, and a commitment to living a life that honors God. Just as Daniel purposed in his heart to not defile himself, we must also purpose in our hearts to set clear moral and spiritual boundaries that protect our relationship with God and help us live a life of conviction. By relying on God's

Word as our guide and being diligent in maintaining our boundaries, we can stay true to our faith and honor God in everything we do.

Chapter 11 - Daring Faith

A heart of conviction, as shown in the life of Daniel, is deeply rooted in daring faith, the kind of faith that leads a person to stand firm in their beliefs even when it's risky or unpopular. Daniel's decision to remain true to his faith, even though it could have cost him his position and his safety, is a powerful example of what it means to have daring faith. In Daniel 1:8, it says, "But Daniel purposed in his heart that he would not defile himself with the portion of the king's meat, nor with the wine which he drank." This choice by Daniel, to refuse the food and wine from the king's table, was not a small act. It was a bold and daring act of faith, made at great personal risk. As a young man living in a foreign land, Daniel was surrounded by the pressures to conform to the customs and ways of Babylon. The food and drink offered to him were part of the royal provisions, and refusing them could have easily been seen as an insult to the king or a refusal to assimilate into the culture of the Babylonian court. Yet, Daniel knew that accepting the king's food would violate the dietary laws given to him by God, and his heart of conviction led him to take a stand, even when it could have cost him everything. This kind of daring faith is what we need today. In a world where standing up for biblical principles is often met with opposition or ridicule, we need the courage and conviction to remain true to our beliefs, no matter the cost.

Daring faith is about more than just believing in God—it's about acting on that belief, even when it's difficult or dangerous. Daniel's decision not to defile himself with the king's food was not made in a vacuum; it was a reflection of his deep trust in God and his unwavering commitment to live according to God's commandments. Daniel wasn't concerned with the opinions of others or with securing his own comfort and safety; his primary concern was honoring God. This teaches us that daring faith requires us to prioritize our relationship with God above all else. It's about choosing to follow God's will, even when it means going against the flow or facing negative consequences. In today's world, where many people are quick to compromise their values in order to fit in or avoid conflict, daring faith means standing firm in what we believe, even when it's unpopular.

One of the most important aspects of daring faith is the willingness to take risks for the sake of our faith. Daniel's refusal to eat the king's food was a risky decision, but it was not the only act of daring faith in his life. Later in the book of Daniel, we see how he continued to practice his faith openly, even when it became illegal to pray to anyone other than the king. In Daniel 6:10, it says, "Now when Daniel knew that the writing was signed, he went into his house; and his windows being open in his chamber toward Jerusalem, he kneeled upon his knees three times a day, and prayed, and gave thanks before his God, as he did aforetime." Daniel knew that by continuing to pray to God, he was risking his life, but his heart of conviction and daring faith led him to do it anyway. This teaches us that daring faith is not about playing it safe—it's about being willing to take risks for the sake of our faith, trusting that God will be with us, no matter the outcome.

In today's world, daring faith is more important than ever. We live in a time when standing up for biblical principles is often met with hostility or opposition. Whether it's in school, at work, in the media, or in our communities, there are many places where expressing our faith or standing firm in our beliefs can lead to criticism, rejection, or even persecution. Yet, Daniel's example shows us that daring faith is not about avoiding conflict or seeking approval from others—it's about staying true to God, even when it's hard. It's about having the courage to stand up for what we know is right, even when others around us are choosing a different path.

Daring faith also requires trust in God's sovereignty. When Daniel refused to eat the king's food or continued to pray to God despite the king's decree, he was placing his trust in God, believing that God would protect him and provide for him. This teaches us that daring faith is about trusting in God's plan, even when we don't know what the outcome will be. It's about believing that God is in control, even in the most difficult circumstances, and that He will take care of us when we choose to stand firm in our faith. In our own lives, we may face situations where standing up for our faith feels risky or where we don't know how things will turn out. But daring faith means trusting that God is with us and that He will honor our faithfulness, even when we can't see the bigger picture.

Another important aspect of daring faith is perseverance. Daniel's daring faith wasn't just a one-time decision—it was a pattern of faithfulness that he demonstrated throughout his life. From his refusal to eat the king's food to his boldness in continuing to pray, Daniel consistently chose to stand firm in his faith, no matter the risks. This teaches us that daring faith is not just about making one bold decision—it's about continually choosing to live with conviction, day after day, in every situation we face. In today's world, where many people are quick to give up or compromise when things get tough, daring faith means persevering in our faith, even when it's hard. It means staying committed to God, even when the challenges and pressures of life try to pull us away from Him.

Daring faith is also about being willing to stand alone. When Daniel made the decision to avoid defiling himself with the king's food, he was setting himself apart from the rest of the young men who were taken to Babylon. He wasn't afraid to be different or to stand out because he knew that his faith in God was more important than fitting in with the crowd. This teaches us that daring faith often requires us to stand alone in our beliefs. In a world where there is constant pressure to conform to societal norms or to go along with what everyone else is doing, daring faith means being willing to stand out and to be different for the sake of our faith. It means having the courage to follow God's ways, even when it makes us unpopular or when others don't understand.

Another key lesson we learn from Daniel's daring faith is that it is rooted in a deep relationship with God. Daniel's boldness in standing up for his beliefs came from his deep trust in God and his unwavering commitment to living a life that honored Him. This teaches us that daring faith is not something we can muster up on our own—it comes from a heart that is deeply connected to God. When we spend time in prayer, studying God's Word, and seeking His guidance, our faith is strengthened, and we are better equipped to stand firm in our beliefs, even when it's difficult. In today's world, where there are so many distractions and competing voices, it's easy to let our relationship with God take a back seat. But Daniel's example reminds us that daring faith is built on a foundation of prayer, study, and a deep relationship with God. The more we rely on God and seek His presence in our lives, the more courageous our faith will become.

Daring faith also requires humility. Daniel's decision to refuse the king's food and to continue praying wasn't about proving his own righteousness or seeking attention—it was about honoring God. This teaches us that daring faith is not about making bold choices for the sake of being bold—it's about living in a way that reflects our commitment to God and His ways. It's about humbling ourselves before God and seeking to honor Him in everything we do. In our own lives, daring faith means being willing to take bold stands for our faith, not for our own glory, but to bring glory to God. It means trusting that God will use our faithfulness to accomplish His purposes, even when we don't fully understand what He is doing.

In conclusion, Daniel's choice to stand firm in his faith, even when it could have cost him his position and safety, is a powerful example of daring faith. His heart of conviction led him to make bold decisions, not out of fear, but out of a deep trust in God and a commitment to honor Him in every area of his life. In today's world, where standing up for biblical principles is often unpopular or risky, we need the same kind of daring faith that Daniel had. We need the courage to stand firm in our beliefs, even when it's difficult, even when it means taking risks, and even when it means standing alone. Daring faith is about trusting in God's sovereignty, persevering in our commitment to Him, and being willing to take bold steps of faith for the sake of His kingdom. Just as Daniel's daring faith led to God's protection and blessing in his life, we can trust that when we choose to stand firm in our faith, God will be with us, guiding us, protecting us, and using our faithfulness to accomplish His purposes in ways we may never fully understand.

Chapter 12 - Divine Focus

A heart of conviction, as demonstrated by Daniel in the Bible, reflects a life rooted in divine focus—a focus that keeps one's heart and mind centered on pleasing God above all else. Daniel's commitment to staying true to God, even when faced with immense pressures and distractions, shows us the power of having a heart that is unwaveringly focused on God's will. In Daniel 1:8, it says, "But Daniel purposed in his heart that he would not defile himself with the portion of the king's meat, nor with the wine which he drank." This decision reveals that Daniel's heart was fixed on pleasing God, even though he was living in a foreign land where the values, customs, and pressures of Babylon were constantly pulling him in a different direction. Daniel's divine focus is a powerful example of how we, too, can live with conviction and purpose in a world filled with distractions. Today, distractions are more plentiful than ever, with technology, social media, busy schedules, and countless other things competing for our attention. But just as Daniel remained focused on pleasing God above all else, we must also cultivate a divine focus in our lives, keeping our hearts and minds centered on God's will, no matter what distractions come our way.

Divine focus is about prioritizing our relationship with God and seeking to honor Him in everything we do. For Daniel, this meant making decisions that aligned with God's commandments, even when it was difficult or when it set him apart from those around him. His refusal to eat the king's food was not just about following dietary laws—it was about making a deliberate choice to honor God in every area of his life. This teaches us that divine focus is about more than just avoiding sin—it's about intentionally seeking to please God in everything we do. It's about making choices that reflect our commitment to His will and our desire to live a life that brings glory to Him. In today's world, where so many things compete for our time and attention, it's easy to get distracted and lose sight of what really matters. But Daniel's example shows us that when our hearts are focused on God, we can navigate the distractions of life and stay true to our faith.

One of the most important aspects of divine focus is keeping our priorities in line with God's will. Daniel could have easily prioritized his position in the king's court, his comfort, or his safety, but instead, he chose to prioritize his relationship with God. This teaches us that divine focus requires us to regularly evaluate our priorities and make sure that God is always at the top of the list. In today's world, where there are so many demands on our time and attention, it can be easy to let other things take precedence over our relationship with God. Whether it's work, school, social activities, or entertainment, there are countless things that can distract us from spending time with God and seeking His will. But divine focus means intentionally making time for God, seeking His presence, and prioritizing His will above all else. It means choosing to spend time in prayer, studying His Word, and seeking His guidance in every decision we make.

Daniel's divine focus was also evident in his prayer life. Throughout the book of Daniel, we see how Daniel consistently sought God in prayer, even when it was dangerous to do so. In Daniel 6:10, it says, "Now when Daniel knew that the writing was signed, he went into his house; and his windows being open in his chamber toward Jerusalem, he kneeled upon his knees three times a day, and prayed, and gave thanks before his God, as he did aforetime." Despite the decree that made it illegal to pray to anyone other than the king, Daniel continued to pray to God three times a day, as he always had. This shows us that divine focus is about consistency and perseverance in our spiritual practices, even when it's difficult. Daniel didn't allow the pressures or dangers around him to distract him from his commitment to God. He remained focused on his relationship with God, no matter the circumstances. This teaches us that divine focus requires discipline and consistency. It's not something that happens automatically—it's something we must cultivate through regular prayer, study of the Bible, and a daily commitment to seeking God's will in every area of our lives.

In today's fast-paced world, where distractions are abundant, it can be easy to become spiritually lazy or to neglect our relationship with God. But Daniel's example reminds us that divine focus is essential for living a life of conviction. Without a heart that is focused on God, it's easy to be swayed by the opinions of others, to get caught up in the busyness of life, or to compromise our values in order to fit in. Divine focus helps us stay grounded in our faith and keeps us aligned with God's will, even when the world around us is pulling us in different directions.

Another important aspect of divine focus is the ability to discern what is truly important. Daniel's decision to avoid defilement by refusing the king's food shows that he understood the spiritual significance of his choices. He recognized that compromising in even small ways could lead him away from God's will. This teaches us that divine focus involves discernment—it's about being able to see beyond the immediate and the superficial, and understanding the deeper spiritual implications of our decisions. In today's world, where so many things are vying for our attention, it's easy to get caught up in things that don't really matter or that can lead us away from God's plan for our lives. But divine focus helps us to stay clear-headed and to make decisions that reflect our commitment to God. It helps us to prioritize what truly matters—our relationship with God and our obedience to His Word—over the temporary distractions of the world.

Divine focus also requires trust in God's plan. Daniel's decision to stay faithful to God, even when it put him at risk, shows that he trusted in God's sovereignty and believed that God's plan was better than anything the world could offer him. This teaches us that divine focus is not just about making good choices—it's about having faith that God's ways are higher than our ways, and trusting Him to guide us, even when we don't understand what He is doing. In our own lives, there will be times when staying focused on God's will means making difficult or unpopular choices. There may be times when the distractions and pressures of the world make it tempting to compromise our faith. But divine focus requires us to trust that God's plan is always best, even when it's hard to see. It means believing that when we stay focused on pleasing God, He will take care of the rest.

Another key lesson we learn from Daniel's divine focus is the importance of not being swayed by external pressures. Daniel was living in a foreign land, surrounded by people who did not share his beliefs or values. The culture of Babylon was very different from what Daniel had grown up with, and there were constant pressures to conform to the ways of the Babylonian court. Yet, Daniel remained focused on God, refusing to let the opinions or expectations of others dictate his choices. This teaches us that divine focus requires us to keep our eyes fixed on God, even when the world around us is pulling us in different directions. In today's world, there are so many voices and influences that try to tell us what we should believe, how we should live, or what we should prioritize. But like Daniel, we must have the courage and conviction to stay focused on God's will, even when it means going against the flow or standing out from the crowd.

Divine focus also involves humility. Daniel's heart was focused on pleasing God, not on seeking recognition or status for himself. Even though Daniel was given a position of influence in the king's court, he remained humble and always gave glory to God for his successes. In Daniel 2:20-21, after interpreting the king's dream, Daniel said, "Blessed be the name of God for ever and ever: for wisdom and might are his: And he changeth the times and the seasons: he removeth kings, and setteth up kings: he giveth wisdom unto the wise, and knowledge to them that know understanding." This shows us that divine focus is about keeping our hearts centered on God's glory, not our own. In a world where people often seek recognition, success, and approval from others, divine focus reminds us that our ultimate goal should be to please God, not to gain the approval of people.

In conclusion, Daniel's heart of conviction and his divine focus on pleasing God above all else is a powerful example for us today. In a world filled with distractions, pressures, and competing voices, we need to cultivate a divine focus that keeps our hearts and minds centered on God's will. Divine focus is about prioritizing our relationship with God, staying consistent in our spiritual practices, and making choices that reflect our commitment to living a life that honors Him. It requires discipline, discernment, trust, and humility, and it helps us stay grounded in our faith, even when the world around us is pulling us in different directions. Just as Daniel remained focused on God, even in the face of pressure and danger, we, too, can live with divine focus, trusting that when we seek to please God above all else, He will guide us, protect us, and use us for His glory.

Conclusion

The story of Daniel, especially in Daniel 1:8 where it says, "But Daniel purposed in his heart that he would not defile himself," teaches us a powerful lesson about living with conviction. Daniel made a deliberate decision to stay faithful to God, even when he was surrounded by a foreign culture that pressured him to compromise. His determination to live according to God's will, regardless of the risks, is an inspiring example of what it means to have a heart of conviction. Daniel didn't wait for the right moment or for things to get easier—he purposed in his heart from the very beginning to honor God, no matter the cost.

As Christians today, we face similar pressures. The world around us often encourages compromise, telling us to follow our own desires or to fit in with society's standards. It's easy to feel overwhelmed, to wonder if standing firm in our faith is even possible in such a challenging environment. But Daniel's story reminds us that living with conviction is not just about a single moment of courage—it's about making daily choices that reflect our commitment to God.

So how do we continue today with a heart of conviction like Daniel? It starts with a decision, just as Daniel purposed in his heart. We must purpose in our hearts to follow Christ fully, no matter the pressures or distractions we face. This means being intentional in our spiritual practices—spending time in prayer, studying God's Word, and surrounding ourselves with fellow believers who encourage us to stay strong in our faith. It also means having the courage to stand up for what is right, even when it's unpopular or when it costs us something.

The life of conviction is not easy, but it is a life of purpose, strength, and trust in God. Daniel's faithfulness led to God's favor and protection, and it showed the world the power of living for God. Today, we are called to that same kind of faithfulness, to live boldly for Christ and to trust that God will guide us through every challenge.

As you go forward from this book, remember Daniel's example and let it inspire you to purpose in your heart to stay true to your faith. Whether in moments of temptation or in the daily decisions that shape your life, choose to honor God in everything you do. A heart of conviction is one that relies on God's strength, seeks His wisdom, and trusts in His promises. Just as Daniel remained steadfast, you too can live a life of conviction that honors God and shines His light in a world that so desperately needs it.

Don't miss out!

Visit the website below and you can sign up to receive emails whenever Joshua Rhoades publishes a new book. There's no charge and no obligation.

https://books2read.com/r/B-A-AJLBB-YDQBF

BOOKS 2 READ

Connecting independent readers to independent writers.

Did you love *A Heart Of Conviction*? Then you should read *Biblical Bravery*[1] by Joshua Rhoades!

[2]

Biblical bravery is a profound concept deeply rooted in the Bible, characterized by unwavering faith, moral integrity, and the courage to act according to divine principles, even when facing adversity or danger. It transcends mere physical courage, encompassing spiritual resilience, ethical steadfastness, and a deep trust in God. This bravery is evident in the lives of biblical figures like David, who faced Goliath with faith in God's deliverance, and Esther, who risked her life to save her people.

At its essence, biblical bravery is grounded in faith— a trust in God's presence, power, and promises. This faith-driven courage compels believers to stand firm in their convictions, regardless of the challenges or threats they may encounter. It also involves moral integrity, exemplified by Joseph's resistance to temptation, choosing righteousness over personal gain.

In today's complex world, the need for biblical bravery is more pressing than ever. Believers are called to uphold their faith, resist societal pressures to conform to secular norms, and advocate for justice and truth. This bravery is not just about grand heroic acts but is also reflected in everyday decisions that align with God's Word, demonstrating a commitment to His principles in all aspects of life.

---

1. https://books2read.com/u/315WL6

2. https://books2read.com/u/315WL6

www.ingramcontent.com/pod-product-compliance
Lightning Source LLC
Chambersburg PA
CBHW021324160726
47994CB00004B/1606